The *American Jou...*

Hands-On History Lab Activities

GLENCOE
McGraw-Hill

New York, New York   Columbus, Ohio   Woodland Hills, California   Peoria, Illinois

To the Teacher

The American Journey Hands-On History Lab Activities provides students with an opportunity to "learn by doing." Students work individually to make items such as candles, a quill pen, or working navigational instruments as their ancestors did it. They prepare foods like peanut butter, and make a solar oven. They make models. History comes alive for students as they work through these activities. Each activity also presents some little-known facts and insights for the historical period.

Glencoe/McGraw-Hill

A Division of The McGraw·Hill Companies

Send all inquiries to:
Glencoe/McGraw-Hill
936 Eastwind Drive
Westerville, Ohio 43081

ISBN 0-02-821807-8

Printed in the United States of America

4 5 6 7 8 9 10 066 02 01 00 99

Customize Your Resources

No matter how you organize your teaching resources, Glencoe has what you need.

The **Teacher's Classroom Resources** for *The American Journey* provides you with a wide variety of supplemental materials to enhance the classroom experience. These resources appear as individual booklets in a carryall tote box. The booklets are designed to open flat so that pages can be easily photocopied without removing them from their booklet. However, if you choose to create separate files, the pages are perforated for easy removal. You may customize these materials using our file folders or tabbed dividers.

The individual booklets and the file management kit supplied in **Teacher's Classroom Resources** give you the flexibility to organize these resources in a combination that best suits your teaching style. Below are several alternatives:

- **Organize all resources by category**
  (all tests, all history themes activities, all cooperative learning activities, etc., filed separately)
- **Organize all resources by category and chapter**
  (all Chapter 1 activities, all Chapter 1 tests, etc.)
- **Organize resources sequentially by lesson**
  (activities, quizzes, readings, etc., for Chapter 1, Chapter 2, and so on)

Table of Contents

Hands-On History Lab Activity 1

Faux Fossils

Paleontologists discovered how life developed by finding small pieces of our past, frozen in time through fossilization. You can create a faux (imitation) fossil using clay and a pit kiln to help you understand how fossils formed.

★ BACKGROUND

Fossils are a record of organisms that lived during prehistoric times. The remains of plants, fish, and animals give scientists an idea of what life was like millions of years ago. Organisms become fossilized when they are buried under layers of earth. Over millions of years, sediment turns them to stone and an image is frozen in time. Usually just the outline of the skeleton remains, but sometimes fossils form quickly enough that that we can see the entire structure.

★ MATERIALS

Tiles:

- low-fire potter's clay, a ball about the size of a grapefruit
- rolling pin
- plant leaves or dried flowers
- table knife
- cutting board
- white chalk
- acrylic matte medium (available in art supply stores)
- soft paintbrush

Pit Kiln:

- shovel
- 1 large grocery bag full of dry sawdust
- rack from barbecue grill
- newspaper
- matches
- metal garbage can lid
- five brick-sized stones or bricks

FASCINATING FACTS

Fossils that carry the first known imprints of vertebrates (organisms that have spines) are 600 million years old!

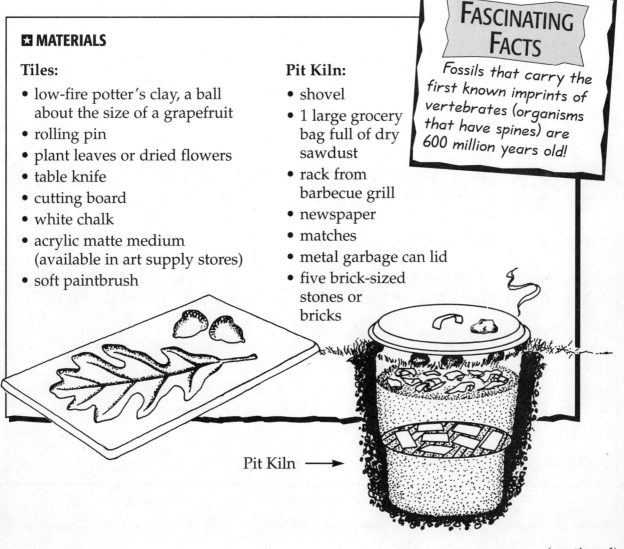

Pit Kiln ⟶

(continued)

Hands-On History Lab Activity 1

☒ WHAT TO DO

A. Knead the clay for 10 minutes to remove air bubbles. Roll the clay out with the rolling pin to ¼″ thickness. Cut the slabs into rectangles about 4″ × 6″.

B. Press a plant part into each clay tile and then lift it off. (If part of the plant sticks, it will burn off during firing.)

C. Place the tiles on the cutting board and allow them to dry until they no longer feel cold to the touch—this will take about a week. Let the tiles dry completely so they don't break when they are fired.

D. To make the pit kiln Dig a circular pit in the ground about 2 feet in diameter and 18 inches deep. Fill the pit with about 3 inches of sawdust and place the grill rack on top of the sawdust. Put the tiles on the rack with 1″ of space around each tile. Fill the rest of the pit with

sawdust. Twist sheets of newspaper into long, thin wicks. Lay the wicks in a single layer on top of the pit. Place four of the stones around the outside edge of the pit. Light the newspaper wicks. *(SAFETY NOTE: Use caution when working with fire. We recommend adult supervision.)* After the newspaper is burning well, place the garbage can lid on the stones and weight it down with the remaining stone. Allow the kiln to burn overnight. It is safe to leave the kiln unattended but keep small children away from the area.

E. After the kiln is cool, take off the lid and remove your tiles from the ashes. Rinse the pottery to remove the remaining ash. Color the surface of the tile with chalk keeping it out of the impressions. Then brush the surface with acrylic matte medium.

LAB ACTIVITY REPORT

1. Explain how fossils are formed in nature. _____

_____

2. What do you think a paleontologist from the future could learn from the fossil tiles you have made? _____

3. Compare your faux fossil imprint to the original leaf or flower. How are they alike? Different? _____

4. Why do you think it takes much longer for natural fossils to occur than it took to make faux fossils? _____

5. How did the clay tiles change after you left them in the pit kiln overnight?

_____

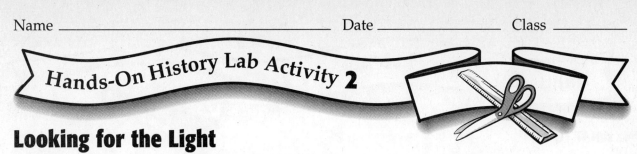

Hands-On History Lab Activity 2

Looking for the Light

Artificial light changed the way we live. Factories can operate at night. Planes, trains, ships, and automobiles can travel easily after dark. Students can do homework at night. It is difficult to imagine what life was like for pioneers without electric lights.

★ BACKGROUND

When the sun set, pioneers reached for candles instead of an electric lamp. Although beeswax made superior candles, colonial Americans made candles from tallow, or animal fats, the only material available to them. They tied a row of candlewicks onto a stick and dipped the wicks into a kettle of hot tallow. A good candle maker could dip between 150 and 200 candles in a day. Because candles were precious, candle makers carefully packed new candles into special boxes and stored them where sunlight could not reach them. Most kitchens had a candle box where a few candles were ready for instant use. You can dip candles as the pioneers did.

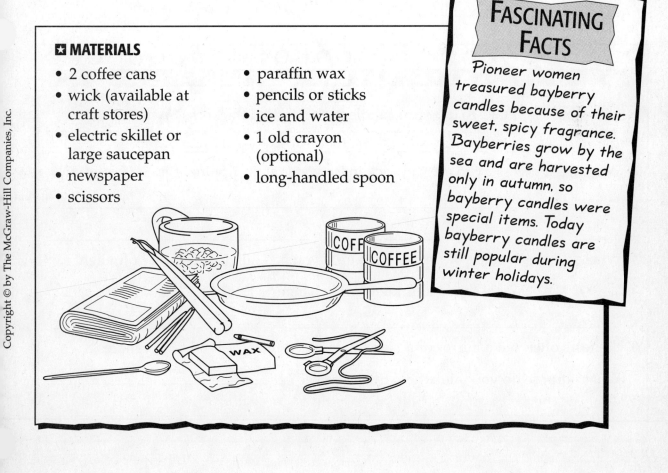

★ MATERIALS

- 2 coffee cans
- wick (available at craft stores)
- electric skillet or large saucepan
- newspaper
- scissors
- paraffin wax
- pencils or sticks
- ice and water
- 1 old crayon (optional)
- long-handled spoon

FASCINATING FACTS

Pioneer women treasured bayberry candles because of their sweet, spicy fragrance. Bayberries grow by the sea and are harvested only in autumn, so bayberry candles were special items. Today bayberry candles are still popular during winter holidays.

(continued)

Hands-On History Lab Activity 2

★ WHAT TO DO

A. Partially fill an electric skillet or saucepan with water. Place small chunks of paraffin in a coffee can to melt. Place the coffee can in the electric skillet or saucepan. Turn the heat on medium. As the wax melts, add additional pieces if necessary to bring the melted wax to a level of 4″ to 6″. If you would like colored candles, add a crayon in the color of your choice and stir with a long-handled spoon. *(SAFETY NOTE: Do not overheat the wax; it may splatter or catch fire.)*

B. Lay newspaper around your work area to catch any drips.

C. Cut wicks 10″ long. (You may use any heavy string if you don't intend to light the candles, but use candlewick if you plan to light the candles.) Tie the wick onto a pencil or a stick. Put ice water in the second coffee can.

D. Briefly dip the wick first into the hot wax and then into the ice water. Continue to dip and cool until the candle reaches the desired thickness. Be sure to dip the candle into the hot wax and remove it very quickly; the wax will begin to melt off the wick if it is left in the hot wax too long or if you let the wax get too hot.

E. When the candle is of the desired thickness, remove the candle from the dipping stick by snipping the wick about ¼″ from the end of the candle.

LAB ACTIVITY REPORT

1. How long did it take to dip your candle to the desired thickness? Why?

_____

2. Why was it necessary to dip the wick in ice water after dipping it in the hot wax?

_____

_____

3. What activities would you have to give up if you had only candlelight or firelight to see by? How do you think your life would change? _____

_____

4. Pioneers often put a mirror or a piece of polished metal behind their candles. What purpose do you think these things served? _____

_____

Hands-On History Lab Activity 3

Floating Boats

The first boat was probably a hollowed-out log. The basic concept has remained the same for hundreds of years. Every boat made today still uses the basic principles discovered by early people. You can experiment with boat making to learn more about these principles.

★ BACKGROUND

If you drop a steel nail into water, it sinks to the bottom. Steel tankers, however, not only stay afloat but also haul heavy materials across the oceans. How is that possible? If you think it has something to do with the air trapped in the ship's hold, you are right. A nail sinks because it is heavier than the water, but a super tanker does not sink because it is filled with air that weighs almost nothing. The steel tanker displaces an amount of water equal to the tanker's weight. As cargo is loaded, the added weight makes the ship sink lower into the water. As long as the ship and cargo weigh less than the water the ship displaces, the ship will float.

★ MATERIALS

- two large plastic dishpans of water
- plasticine clay (other modeling clays will not work)
- toothpicks, matchsticks, or coffee stirrers
- small pieces of paper
- scissors
- spoon and table knife, to shape your boats
- marbles
- paper clips
- 1¼ cups salt
- notebook to record observations

FASCINATING FACTS

Early sailors used to suffer from scurvy, a disease caused by a lack of vitamin C in shipboard diets. When British sailors learned that eating limes, which are rich in vitamin C, prevented this disease, limes became part of the ships' food supply. British sailors came to be called limeys, a nickname that is still used today.

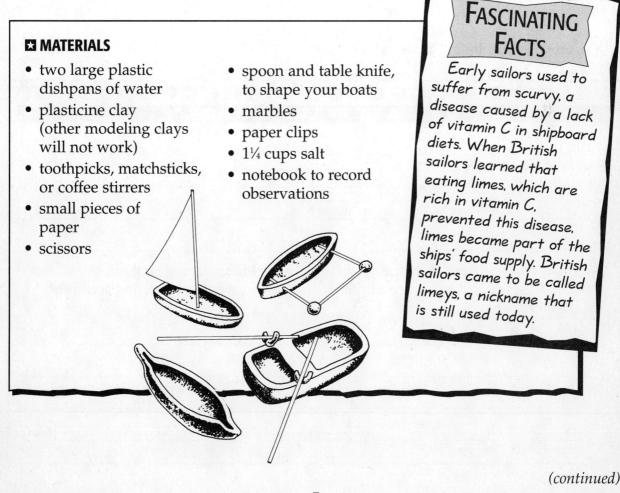

(continued)

Hands-On History Lab Activity 3

✦ WHAT TO DO

A. Fill each dishpan about three-quarters full with water, keeping track of how many quarts of water you use in each pan. In one of the dishpans, add 1¼ cups salt for each quart of water. Form the plasticine into two balls, about the size of golf balls. Drop one ball into the freshwater and one into the salt water. **In your notebook write down what happens in each dishpan.**

B. Now take the balls of clay and form them into small, relatively flat boats. **Will these boats float? Do they float better in freshwater or salt water? Why? Write your observations in the notebook.** Take small objects, such as marbles and paper clips, and place them in each of your boats. **Record your observations. Which boat holds the most weight before it sinks?**

C. Research to find some pictures of different kinds of boats and mold the plasticine into different boat shapes such as canoes, catamarans, sailboats, and so on. Cut sails out of small pieces of paper and use toothpicks as masts for your sailboats. Create as many different kinds of boats as you can. **Make notes on which shapes float best.** Add weights such as marbles and paper clips. **Which boat holds the most weight?**

D. Build the biggest boat that you can that will still float in your container. **What is the shape of this boat?** Build the smallest boat that you can that will still hold a marble. **What design worked best for this boat? Record your observations.**

LAB ACTIVITY REPORT

1. Did the boats generally float higher in the salt water or the freshwater? Explain why you think this was so. _____

_____

_____

2. Write a synopsis of which type of boat works best for carrying cargo in salt water and in freshwater. Also, write a brief passage about what you learned about the design of boats.

_____

_____

_____

_____

Hands-On History Lab Activity 4

Water Wheeling

Waterwheels change the energy of falling water into mechanical energy that can be used for running machinery. Try to create a waterwheel to see how our ancestors harnessed the power of water.

★ BACKGROUND

Waterwheels once turned heavy millstones that ground grain into flour. The turning millwheel, through a series of gears, turned two large, flat stones that crushed the grain between them. The rotation pushed the flour to the edges. Waterwheels also provided power for blacksmiths, paper makers, and lumberyards.

★ MATERIALS

- 12 plastic cups, 3-oz. size
- 2 plastic plates, 8" or 9" size
- 2 empty thread spools
- masking tape, 1" wide
- scissors
- ruler
- dishpan
- 2 one pound coffee cans filled with stones

- 2 yardsticks
- 12 rubber bands
- water pitcher
- 18" piece of stiff wire, a coat hanger will work
- household cement
- pliers for wire cutting
- one large, 3" nail
- ⅛" drill

FASCINATING FACTS

In Europe water-wheels first appeared in early medieval times. In the mid-1800s, more than 20,000 mills powered by waterwheels operated in England alone.

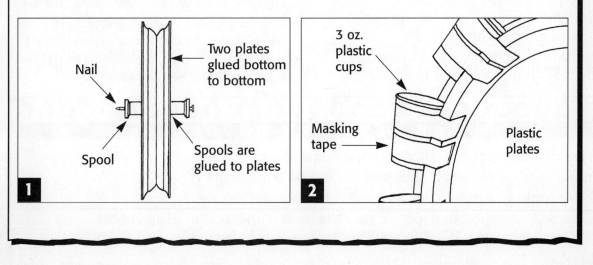

1. Nail — Spool — Two plates glued bottom to bottom — Spools are glued to plates

2. 3 oz. plastic cups — Masking tape — Plastic plates

(continued)

Hands-On History Lab Activity 4

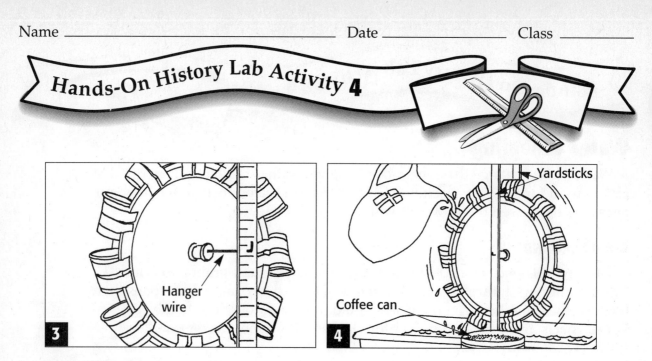

★ WHAT TO DO

A. Nest the two plates together and punch a hole through the center of both plates. Then use household cement to glue the plates together, bottom to bottom. Spread cement on one end of each spool, and glue one spool on each plate, aligning the holes in the plates with the holes in the spools. Push the large nail all the way through the holes while the glue dries (about ½ hour.) **(See diagram 1.)** While you wait for the glue to dry, build a stand for the waterwheel. **(See diagram 4.)**

B. Hold one of the yardsticks upright against one of the rock-filled coffee cans and secure with 6 rubber bands. Repeat with the other yardstick and filled coffee can. Then place the cans on opposite sides of the dishpan.

C. Drill a ⅛" hole through each yardstick, about 7" above the top of the dishpan.

D. Straighten a wire coat hanger and using the pliers, cut a length of wire 2" longer than the distance between the two yardsticks.

E. When the glue has dried on the plates, tape each cup to the rim of the joined plates with 2, 8" strips of masking tape, about ½" apart. Adjust slightly for even spacing. Remove the nail from the holes in the spools and plates. **(See diagram 2.)**

F. Bend up ½" at one end of the the coat hanger wire with the pliers. Insert the straight end of the wire through the holes in the yardstick, the waterwheel, and then the other yardstick. Then bend up about ½" of the straight end to secure the waterwheel. **(See diagram 3.)**

G. Fill the pitcher with water. Slowly pour the water over the waterwheel so that water fills each of the cups to make the wheel rotate. **(See diagram 4.)**

LAB ACTIVITY REPORT

Answer the following questions on a separate sheet of paper.

1. Which part of the wheel should the water be pointed at? Why?

2. How could you make your waterwheel spin faster? Slower?

3. On a separate sheet of paper, draw a diagram with labels to explain how a waterwheel works. Why do you think waterwheels are rarely used today?

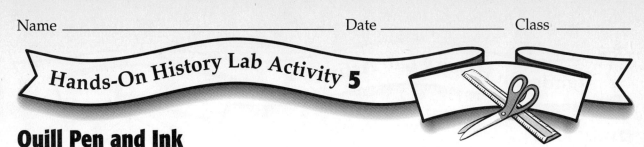

Hands-On History Lab Activity 5

Quill Pen and Ink

From the 1500s until the 1800s, most people wrote documents using quill pens, made from the large feathers of geese or swans. Try to make a quill pen and natural inks, and you can write and draw as our ancestors did.

★ BACKGROUND

Beautiful handwriting was important in the 1800s. Letters were more than just a means of communication. They were an expression of special regard for the people who received them. The more detailed the handwriting the better. Children and adults often wrote in diaries called monitors. They recorded the weather or daily activities, but rarely revealed their thoughts and feelings. Ink was not always available so writers made it from such things as walnut shells or berries. Because these inks faded over time, original documents are often hard to find and read. Pens, too, were homemade.

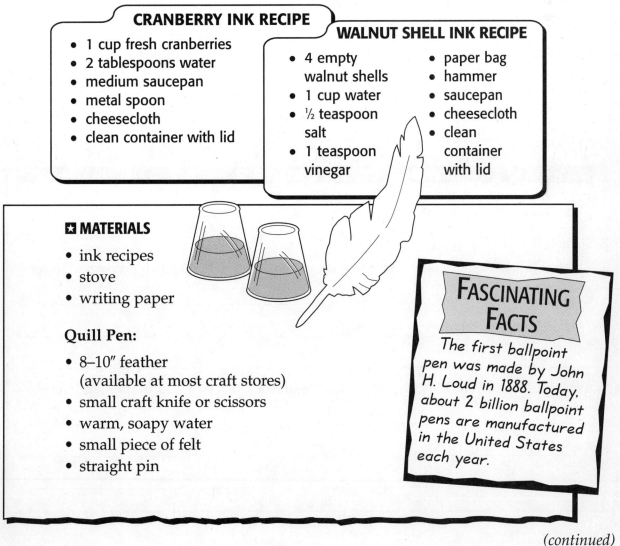

CRANBERRY INK RECIPE

- 1 cup fresh cranberries
- 2 tablespoons water
- medium saucepan
- metal spoon
- cheesecloth
- clean container with lid

WALNUT SHELL INK RECIPE

- 4 empty walnut shells
- 1 cup water
- ½ teaspoon salt
- 1 teaspoon vinegar
- paper bag
- hammer
- saucepan
- cheesecloth
- clean container with lid

★ MATERIALS

- ink recipes
- stove
- writing paper

Quill Pen:

- 8–10" feather (available at most craft stores)
- small craft knife or scissors
- warm, soapy water
- small piece of felt
- straight pin

FASCINATING FACTS

The first ballpoint pen was made by John H. Loud in 1888. Today, about 2 billion ballpoint pens are manufactured in the United States each year.

(continued)

Hands-On History Lab Activity 5

★ WHAT TO DO

A. To make cranberry ink Place the cranberries and water in a saucepan. Bring the mixture to a boil. *(SAFETY NOTE: Handle hot materials carefully to avoid burns.)* Crush the cranberries with the spoon to release their color. Allow the mixture to cool. Place a piece of cheesecloth over the container. Carefully pour the mixture into the container. The cheesecloth will strain out the crushed cranberries. Seal with a lid.

B. To make walnut shell ink Place the shells in a paper bag and crush them with the hammer. Put the crushed shells in the saucepan and add the water. Bring the mixture to a boil. Add the salt and vinegar to set the ink. Turn down the heat and allow the mixture to simmer for 30 minutes. Cool. Strain the ink through the cheesecloth into the

container. Keep the mixture tightly covered and avoid getting it on your clothes or hands. It stains.

C. To make a quill pen Soak the feather in warm soapy water for 15 minutes. Trim about 2″ of feathers off along the shaft at the bottom end of the feather. Cut off the end of the feather's shaft at an angle to form the nib, or point, of the pen. *(SAFETY NOTE: Cut on heavy cardboard and handle sharp tools with care to avoid cuts.)* Use a straight pin to clean out the inside of the quill. Be careful not to crack the nib. Cut a small slit in the center of the nib to help control the ink flow. Dip the nib into ink, blot on a small piece of felt, and you are ready to write.

D. Practice with your quill pen and homemade inks on a sheet of writing paper.

LAB ACTIVITY REPORT

1. What color ink did the walnut shells make? _____

2. Which kind of ink worked the best in your tests? _____

3. Do you think it would take you much longer to do your homework if you had to use

quill pens and homemade inks? Why? _____

_____

_____

4. Was your handwriting neater or messier with the quill pen and homemade inks?

_____

_____

_____

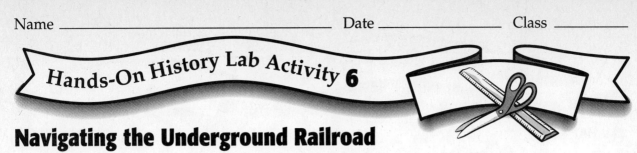

Hands-On History Lab Activity 6

Navigating the Underground Railroad

The Underground Railroad helped enslaved people escape to the North and Canada. Often the runaway's only guidance came from the North Star. A cross staff uses the North Star to help with navigation. You can make a cross staff and learn to use it.

✪ BACKGROUND

The Underground Railroad's most heavily traveled routes ran through Ohio, Indiana, and Pennsylvania. Although no formal records exist, historians think at least 10,000 people escaped enslavement using the Underground Railroad.

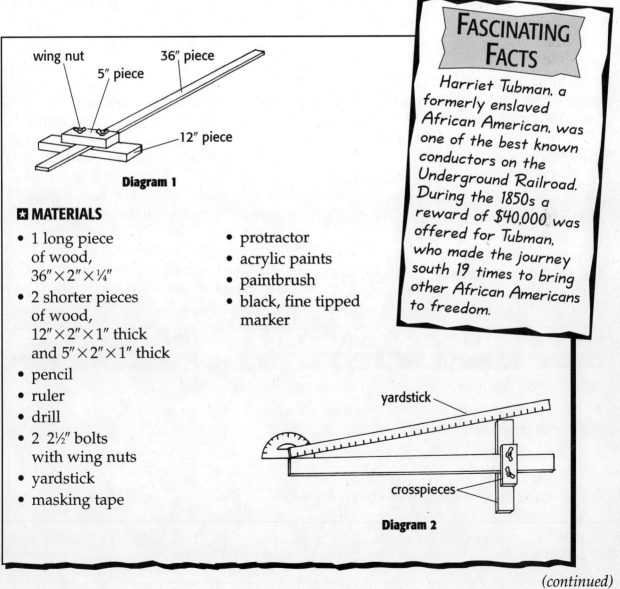

wing nut   36" piece
5" piece
12" piece

Diagram 1

✪ MATERIALS

- 1 long piece of wood, 36" × 2" × ¼"
- 2 shorter pieces of wood, 12" × 2" × 1" thick and 5" × 2" × 1" thick
- pencil
- ruler
- drill
- 2 2½" bolts with wing nuts
- yardstick
- masking tape

- protractor
- acrylic paints
- paintbrush
- black, fine tipped marker

> ### FASCINATING FACTS
>
> Harriet Tubman, a formerly enslaved African American, was one of the best known conductors on the Underground Railroad. During the 1850s a reward of $40,000 was offered for Tubman, who made the journey south 19 times to bring other African Americans to freedom.

yardstick
crosspieces

Diagram 2

(continued)

Hands-On History Lab Activity 6

☒ WHAT TO DO

A. Mark the center of the 5″ piece of wood, using a ruler. Lay the 36″ piece of wood over the mark to form a cross. Draw lines onto the 5″ piece of wood, using the edges of the 36″ piece as a guide. Draw 2 large dots just outside the lines centering them at the midpoint of each line.

B. Drill a hole large enough for the bolts to fit through at each of the large dots. *(SAFETY NOTE: Wear safety glasses if using power tools.)* Mark the location for matching holes on the 12″ piece of wood. Remove the 5″ piece of wood and set it aside. Drill holes in the spots you marked on the 12″ piece.

C. Place the 36″ piece of wood between the two smaller pieces and insert the bolts into the proper holes. **(See diagram 1.)** Place the wing nuts on the bolts and tighten.

D. Lay the staff on the ground as shown in diagram 2 and loosen the nuts. Slide the crosspieces down to about 5½″ from the bottom of the 36″ stick. Place the protractor at the other end of the stick, as shown in diagram 2, and tape it with masking tape. Place the yardstick as shown. Slide the crosspiece down until the yardstick lies along the 10° line on the protractor. Draw a line across the surface of the 36″ piece of the cross staff at this point. Continue sliding the crosspiece down, marking every 5°. You should be able to mark degrees up to 65° or more.

E. Take the instrument apart. Paint a different color for every section marked on the stick. After the paint dries, remark the numbers and degrees.

F. Use the cross staff at night. **(See diagram 3.)** Loosen the wing nuts so the crosspiece moves smoothly. Hold on to the crosspiece. Extend your arm with the longest piece of the cross staff at eye level and parallel to the ground. The higher numbers on the cross staff should be closest to your nose. Point the cross staff at the North Star, the brightest star in the northern sky. Slide the crosspiece until it lines up with your line of sight. Read the number closest to where the cross piece rests on the marked wood. This is the altitude of the star and the latitude where you are.

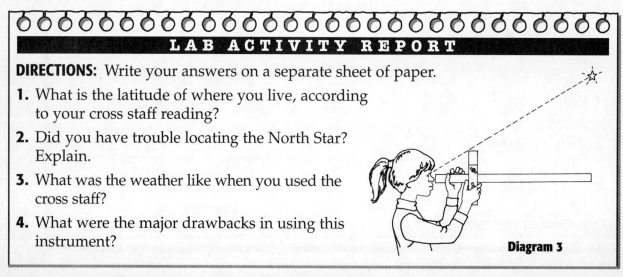

LAB ACTIVITY REPORT

DIRECTIONS: Write your answers on a separate sheet of paper.

1. What is the latitude of where you live, according to your cross staff reading?
2. Did you have trouble locating the North Star? Explain.
3. What was the weather like when you used the cross staff?
4. What were the major drawbacks in using this instrument?

Diagram 3

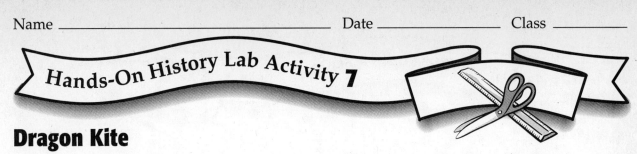

Hands-On History Lab Activity 7

Dragon Kite

For more than 2,000 years the people of China and other Asian countries have been flying kites. You can make a dragon kite and experiment with air currents.

★ BACKGROUND

During the 1700s kites proved that air is colder at higher altitudes; they also gave Benjamin Franklin the shock of his life. In 1752 Franklin discovered that lightning was electricity using a kite during a thunderstorm. In the 1800s the first men flew with the help of six kites tied together, and the box kite inspired Wilbur and Orville Wright's first plane. Flying kites helps you understand air currents.

★ MATERIALS

- poster board
- scissors
- stapler
- colored tissue paper
- white chalk
- ruler
- black marker
- rubber cement

- 11 very thin bamboo wands or very thin dowels, 26" long
- hole punch
- kite string
- cardboard box, about 24" × 40"

FASCINATING FACTS

Koreans have a sport called kite fighting. The kite fliers apply a mixture of glue and sand or glass to the kite string. When opponents' strings cross, the rough strings saw at each other. The first kite to be set free when the string breaks loses.

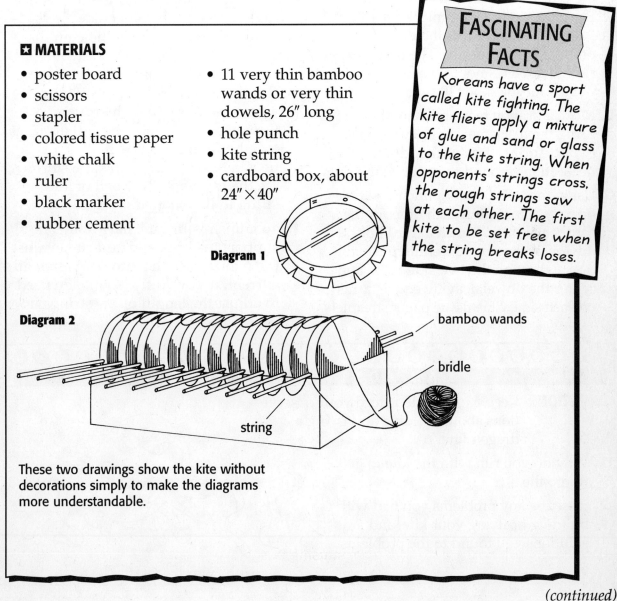

Diagram 1

Diagram 2

bamboo wands

bridle

string

These two drawings show the kite without decorations simply to make the diagrams more understandable.

(continued)

Hands-On History Lab Activity 7

✖ WHAT TO DO

A. Cut the poster board into 11 strips—28″ long and 1″ wide. Form each strip into a ring and staple. Lay out a piece of tissue paper and place one ring on the paper. Using the white chalk, trace a circle 1″ out from the ring. Cut out the circle. Create tabs to glue onto the ring by making 1″ deep cuts every 2″ around the edge of the cut out circle. **(See diagram 1.)**

B. Spread rubber cement or glue around the outside of the poster board ring. Place the ring in the center of the tissue paper circle and press the glue tabs up onto the glued surface. The tissue paper should stretch smoothly across the ring. Repeat for the other 10 rings.

C. Make a dragon face on one of the rings using the black marker or cut out tissue paper. Add ruffles or other dragon-like decorations around the edge of the ring.

D. Using the hole punch, punch two holes directly across from each other in the cardboard rings. Punch a third hole at the top of the ring. Carefully push a dowel through the two side holes and center the dowel, leaving equal "arms" on each side. Glue tissue paper streamers to the ends of the dowel. Repeat the process with all of the rings.

E. Cut kite strings into 30 pieces, 8″ long. To assemble the kite, put the rings with arms across a cardboard box in the order you prefer, spacing them 4″ to 6″ apart. **(See diagram 2.)** Start at the first ring and tie a string around the arm. Connect that arm to the arm on the next ring. Continue until all of the rings connect on one side. Repeat the process on the other side. Then tie a string through the top hole on the first ring. Connect to the next ring's top hole until all of the rings connect. Cut three pieces of string 12″ long. Tie a piece of string to each arm and one through the top hole. Bring the strings together in front of the first ring and tie a knot. This forms the kite's bridle. Tie the free end of the ball of kite string to the knotted area.

F. To launch your kite, have someone support the back end and run against the wind. Once the kite catches an air current, it should fly. You made need to adjust the length of the strings in the bridle.

🔘🔘🔘🔘🔘🔘🔘🔘🔘🔘🔘🔘🔘🔘🔘🔘🔘🔘🔘🔘🔘🔘🔘🔘🔘🔘🔘🔘🔘🔘🔘🔘

LAB ACTIVITY REPORT

DIRECTIONS: Keep a journal to record your observations about building and flying a dragon kite.

1. Why do you run with the kite to get it into the air?

2. Describe any problems you had with building or flying your kite, and any solutions you found to the problems.

Name _____ Date _____ Class _____

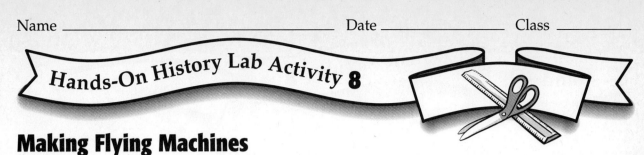
Making Flying Machines

The principles of flight remain the same for a fighter pilot, a paper airplane maker, or a bird. You can create paper airplanes to help you understand the principles of flight.

★ BACKGROUND

Scientists studied birds for hundreds of years and dreamed of one day soaring through the air. The airplane, paper airplane, and bird all have wings and a tail and must have speed to keep their lift. The first plane that maintained flight, though, looked more like a giant box kite than a bird. Orville and Wilbur Wright's gas-powered flying machine lifted off at Kitty Hawk, North Carolina, in 1903, and flew just 120 feet. The Wright's plane still has much in common with today's jets, however.

A pilot's ability to steer the plane is crucial. Flaps operated from the cockpit of the plane help the pilot control it. Elevators on the bottom of the plane's tail control elevation and the rudder on the tail's top controls the direction of turns. Watch to see how the wings, elevators, and rudders affect the flight of your planes.

★ MATERIALS FOR THREE PLANES

- several sheets of 8½″ × 11″ paper
- scissors
- tape
- plastic drinking straw

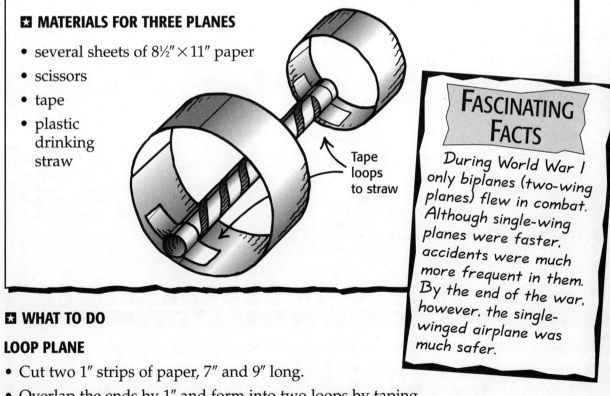

Tape loops to straw

FASCINATING FACTS

During World War I only biplanes (two-wing planes) flew in combat. Although single-wing planes were faster, accidents were much more frequent in them. By the end of the war, however, the single-winged airplane was much safer.

★ WHAT TO DO

LOOP PLANE

- Cut two 1″ strips of paper, 7″ and 9″ long.
- Overlap the ends by 1″ and form into two loops by taping the ends together. Tape the loops to the straw. **(See diagram above.)**
- Fly the plane with the smaller loop facing forward.

(continued)

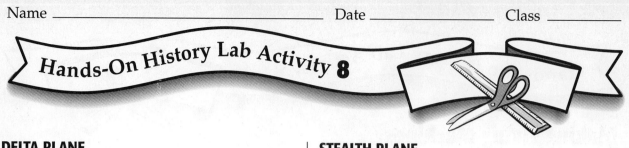

Hands-On History Lab Activity 8

DELTA PLANE

Fold an 8½″ × 11″ piece of paper according to the diagrams. Fly the Delta airplane. Adjust the rudder and elevators to see what happens.

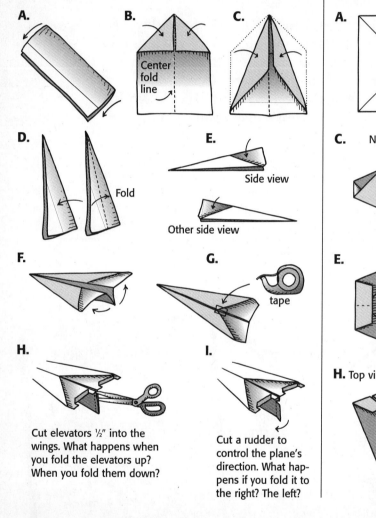

A.

B. Center fold line

C.

D. Fold

E. Side view

Other side view

F.

G. tape

H. Cut elevators ½″ into the wings. What happens when you fold the elevators up? When you fold them down?

I. Cut a rudder to control the plane's direction. What happens if you fold it to the right? The left?

STEALTH PLANE

Fold a square 8½″ × 8½″ piece of paper according to the diagrams. Fly the Stealth airplane. Adjust the rudder and elevators to see what happens.

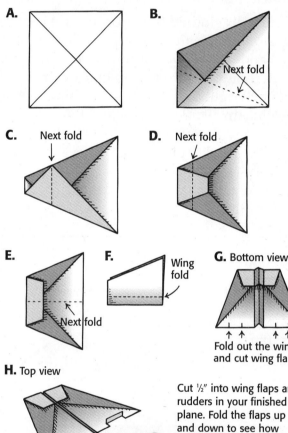

A.

B. Next fold

C. Next fold

D. Next fold

E. Next fold

F. Wing fold

G. Bottom view
Fold out the wings and cut wing flaps.

H. Top view

Cut ½″ into wing flaps and rudders in your finished plane. Fold the flaps up and down to see how the elevators affect the plane's flight.

LAB ACTIVITY REPORT

DIRECTIONS: Write your observations on a separate sheet of paper.

1. Keep notes on the ways you varied the flight of your planes, recording what happened when you adjusted the elevators and rudders in different ways. What did you learn about controlling an airplane from your models?

Hands-On History Lab Activity 9

Making and Using a Barometer

The weather is important. We try to predict the weather for reasons as simple as knowing if we need to wear a coat to school or as complex as deciding whether to launch or land the space shuttle. One instrument we use to predict the weather is the barometer. During World War II the barometer and other instruments helped predict the best time for bombing runs. You can make a barometer and try your luck at predicting the weather.

✪ BACKGROUND

The Italian physicist Evangelista Torricelli invented the barometer, an instrument for measuring the air pressure. Barometer comes from the Greek words: *baros* meaning "heaviness or weight" and *metron* meaning "to measure." Observers saw that the rise and fall of the air pressure coincided with changes in the weather. Areas of high pressure brought good weather; low pressure brought clouds and rain.

World War II planes were more sensitive to the weather than modern aircraft because they did not fly above the weather as today's jets can. Watching the barometer helped the Army Air Corps predict if the weather would be suitable for bombing runs. If the Air Corps predicted a storm, a bombing run could be postponed. Pilots also use a barometer, called a pressure altimeter, to determine altitude.

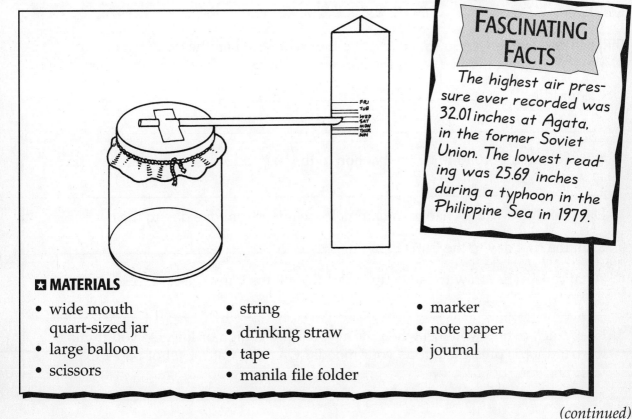

FASCINATING FACTS

The highest air pressure ever recorded was 32.01 inches at Agata, in the former Soviet Union. The lowest reading was 25.69 inches during a typhoon in the Philippine Sea in 1979.

✪ MATERIALS

- wide mouth quart-sized jar
- large balloon
- scissors

- string
- drinking straw
- tape
- manila file folder

- marker
- note paper
- journal

(continued)

Hands-On History Lab Activity 9

★ WHAT TO DO

A. Cut off the neck of the balloon and stretch the remaining rubber over the mouth of the jar. The surface should be as flat and smooth as possible. Tie the balloon to the neck of the jar with string. The balloon should be held firmly in place. Trim both ends of the straw at an angle. Tape the straw onto the balloon to form a pointer. **(See the diagram.)**

B. Use the manila file folder to create a column for recording the movement of the pointer. Cut the folder down the center seam. Fold the folder lengthwise into thirds. Tape at the open seam to create a triangular shaped column. Stand the column next to the jar with the straw pointing to, but not touching the column. Mark and date a line where the straw is

pointing. On a separate sheet of paper, make a note of the weather conditions on that date and at that time. Check the barometer every few hours. Mark a date and time line to indicate where the straw is pointing.

C. Make notes in a journal to keep track of the readings on the barometer and the weather conditions. Continue to check the barometer for a week. Each time the straw is at a new place, mark the column with the date and time and note the weather in your journal. You should begin to see a pattern. When the straw points downward, for example, the weather will have certain characteristics. If the barometer's pointer is rising, the weather will have other characteristics.

LAB ACTIVITY REPORT

DIRECTIONS: Using your journal, describe the weather when the barometer is up.

1. What is the weather like when the barometer is down? When the barometer is in

the middle? _____

_____

2. Why was it important to tie the balloon to the jar? _____

_____

3. Did you find a wider change in barometer reading from one day to the next or

from the first day to the last? _____

4. What causes the straw to move up and down on the barometer? _____

_____

5. Keep track of how you feel when the air pressure is high or low. Do you think the barometric pressure affects your moods? On a separate sheet of paper explain your answer.

Hands-On History Lab Activity 10

Peanut Butter Mania

Every second someone in the United States or Canada buys a jar of peanut butter. Try making one of America's favorite spreads the old-fashioned way.

★ BACKGROUND

When the boll weevil, an insect that attacks cotton plants, damaged cotton crops after the Civil War, Southern farmers began to look for a substitute crop. They planted peanuts on more and more acres and researchers looked for new uses for peanuts. In 1890 a doctor who was looking for an easily digestible form of protein for his patients made peanut butter, and the rest, as they say, is history. The peanut butter sandwich became a permanent part of the American diet. Of the 4 billion pounds of peanuts the United States produces each year, half become peanut butter. Even if you don't live in one of the major peanut-producing states of Georgia, Alabama, North Carolina, Texas, Oklahoma, Virginia, and Florida, you can make your own peanut butter. Try making two different batches and compare the results.

★ MATERIALS FOR EACH BATCH

- 1 cup shelled peanuts
- 1½ tablespoons peanut oil
- ½ teaspoon salt
- blender or food processor
- heavy rolling pin
- 2 1-quart heavy plastic bags with zipper type closings
- spatula
- plastic container with lid
- crackers or celery
- 1 teaspoon cinnamon (optional)
- ¼ cup honey (optional)

FASCINATING FACTS

By the time you graduate from high school, you will probably have eaten about 1,500 peanut butter sandwiches.

(continued)

Hands-On History Lab Activity 10

◪ WHAT TO DO

A. Batch One: Place the peanuts in a blender. Blend for about one minute, or until peanuts are finely chopped. Add the oil and salt and blend until smooth.
Batch Two: Put a cup of peanuts into a plastic bag. Close the bag securely. Then place that bag inside a similar bag, so your peanuts are double bagged. Use the rolling pin to crush the peanuts inside the plastic bag, rolling until they are crushed. Then open the bags and add the oil and salt. Try to remove as much air as possible from the bag. Continue rolling until the peanut butter is of spreading consistency.

B. Try your peanut butter on a cracker or celery stick. Place the remaining peanut butter into covered containers. These peanut butters need to be refrigerated. The oil will separate from the crushed peanuts. Stir well before using to get the best consistency and taste.

C. You can add ¼ cup of honey after grinding the nuts. Just blend into the peanut butter. Or you can try adding a teaspoon of cinnamon to the peanut butter for a different taste. Keep notes of how these ingredients affected the taste and texture of your peanut butter.

LAB ACTIVITY REPORT

DIRECTIONS: Answer the following questions in the space provided.

1. How much peanut butter did you make from 1 cup of peanuts? _____

2. How would you describe the peanut butter made by each method? _____
_____
_____

3. Did you add honey to either batch of peanut butter? If so did it change the texture of the peanut butter? _____
_____

4. How would you describe the differences between your peanut butters and the peanut butter you buy? _____
_____

5. How do you think making peanut butter commercially affected peanut butter's popularity? _____

Hands-On History Lab Activity 11

Drying Food

Food that goes on the space shuttle is often dried, and water is added in space to reestablish the food to a more edible form. Storage space in a spacecraft is very limited and refrigeration is not always available. You can have a taste of space food by making a food dryer to prepare foods of the kind that travel into space.

★ BACKGROUND

Food on early spacecrafts was compressed, processed, and packaged to take up the least amount of room possible. During the first manned space flights, astronauts knew that food was to be endured, not enjoyed. With longer space flights, however, unpleasant or tasteless food can lower morale. Dietitians and astronauts with space experience now test a variety of dried foods to plan a balanced, tasty diet. Once in space, astronauts need about 3,000 calories and 2.5 quarts of water each day—more than most people on Earth need.

★ MATERIALS

- cardboard box, 12″×18″×24″, available at shipping stores (One end should be open.)
- utility knife
- aluminum foil
- clear tape
- black plastic tape
- clear plastic wrap
- one yard of cheesecloth or window screen
- paintbrush
- apples, pears, or any other fruits or vegetables you would like to dry
- yardstick
- 2 cooling racks, such as those used for cookies or cakes
- black paint
- pencil

FASCINATING FACTS

Some items developed specifically for space use are now part of our everyday lives, such as Tang orange drink and pop-tops on beverage cans.

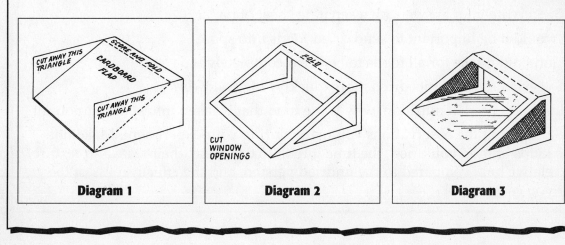

Diagram 1

Diagram 2

Diagram 3

Name _____ Date _____ Class _____

Hands-On History Lab Activity 11

★ WHAT TO DO

A. Lay the box down on one of its large sides. Measure 2″ from the back corner of the closed end of the box. Starting at this point, cut along the corner fold with the utility knife from your mark to the front corner. *(SAFETY NOTE: Utility knives are very sharp; take care to avoid cuts.)* Repeat the same process on the opposite side. Lay the yardstick across the back of the box in line with the two previous cuts and score a line along the yardstick. Scoring means to cut through the first layer of cardboard only, creating a line that you can bend easily to make a flap.

B. Bend the cardboard flap down so that it touches the bottom of the box. **(See diagram 1.)** Then with the pencil, trace a line along both edges of the flap on the inside of the box. Tip the box on first one side and then the other to cut along the angled lines with the utility knife. The bottom edge should be even. **(See diagram 1.)** Measure in 1½″ around the edges of the top and sides of the box, as though you were creating a frame. **(See diagram 2.)** Use the utility

knife to carefully cut out the middle of the frames, creating windows.

C. Cover the entire inside of the box, except for the windows, with aluminum foil, fastening the foil with clear tape. Using black plastic tape, tape the screen or cheesecloth over the side windows. The top window should be covered with clear plastic wrap. Tape two pieces of plastic wrap together if necessary. Use black plastic tape to fasten the plastic wrap to the top. **(See diagram 3.)** Paint all of the outside cardboard with black paint and allow it to dry.

D. Place the racks in the dryer. Place thinly sliced fruit or vegetables on the racks. Close the dryer and place it in a warm, sunny spot either inside or outside. The less humid it is, the quicker the fruits or vegetables will dry. Usually the food will be completely dry after two weeks. Make sure the dryer does not get rained on and take it inside at night when dew forms.

LAB ACTIVITY REPORT

DIRECTIONS: Write your answers on a separate sheet of paper.

1. Why would it be important to send dried foods into space?

2. How long did it take for all foods to be dried completely?

3. What vegetables and fruits dried more quickly? More slowly?

4. In addition to needed nutrition, why is the food that is taken into space important?

5. Write a report of the observations you made during your experiment. Make note of the kinds of food you dried, the time it took to dry them, their taste and texture, their relative bulk compared to the undried version, and the effectiveness of the dryer you constructed.

Answer Key

⊞ ACTIVITY 1

1. Fossils are created when organisms are covered with sediment, which pressure gradually turns to stone, leaving an impression of the organism in the stone.

2. Answers will vary, but students should mention the types of plants found in their area and what these plants might show about the climate of their region.

3. Answers will vary, but students might note that their fossils preserved the general shape of the plant and some of its texture, but it did not convey color, hardness or softness, or give an indication if the plant had the same shape on both sides.

4. Fossils can take thousands or millions of years to form because many conditions need to be present in order for fossilization to occur. The organism must die in a location where it is buried under silt or sediment, successive layers must build up over the sediment to create pressure; the organism must fossilize rather than decay due to the conditions. When students made their faux fossils, they created conditions artificially, but fossils must wait for nature to take its course.

5. Students should note that the fired tiles are harder, darker, and stronger.

⊞ ACTIVITY 2

1. Answers will vary from student to student. Students might note that it took longer than they expected. The actual time will vary because variations in wicks, wax, and individual dipping rhythms will affect the speed of candle dipping.

2. If the wax wasn't cooled between dips, it would melt when it was dipped in the hot wax and no wax would accumulate to form the candle.

3. Answers will vary but could include reading, homework, playing sports. Look for evidence of thought beyond the obvious answers. Changes in lifestyle could include an earlier bedtime or more time spent with family.

4. Mirrors and polished metal reflected more of the candles' light into the room. Since candlelight is very dim and candles we re expensive, pioneers needed to make the best use of what light they had.

⊞ ACTIVITY 3

Journal Observations

- Students will observe that the balls of plasticine sank in both pans of water.

- When the balls of plasticine are formed into boats, they will float; the boat in the pan containing salt water will float better because the salt water is denser.

- Boats can carry more weight in salt water because it is denser than freshwater.

- Deeper boats can carry more weight than shallower boats of the same size.

- Narrower boats with sails tend to tip more easily than wider boats.

- Observations on the kinds of boats and their characteristics will vary depending on the kinds of boats students may create.

1. The boats should float higher in salt water. Salt water is denser than freshwater, so it can carry more weight.

2. Answers will vary but should show careful observations and evidence of reasoning and critical thinking.

⊞ ACTIVITY 4

1. The water should be pointed at the top of the wheel because the cups at the top will be heavier when they are filled with water, so gravity will pull them down, causing the wheel to turn.

2. The wheel will turn faster as the amount of water pouring over the cups increases and the cups fill faster.

3. Student diagrams should be based on the following principle: the weight of the water turns the wheel which in turn can turn gears that put other objects in motion. Waterwheels are rarely used today because more efficient forms of power now grind grains and do other work. Waterwheels are limited in where they can be used because they need falling water to operate. Many developing countries, however, use variations of the waterwheel to provide power.

★ ACTIVITY 5

1. Walnut shells make brown ink.

2. walnut shell ink

3. Answers will vary but should recognize how improvements in writing instruments have changed the way information is recorded.

4. Answers will vary, but students will probably find writing is messier with a quill pen.

★ ACTIVITY 6

1. Answers will vary. Students' measurements with the cross staff may vary slightly from the actual location, but students should verify their readings by consulting a map.

2. Answers will vary. Some students will find it easy to locate the North Star. Others may find it more difficult.

3. Answers will vary according to local conditions.

4. Although the cross staff was better than nothing, it did have drawbacks. It could be used only at night; human error was common; it could help determine latitude, but not longitude.

★ ACTIVITY 7

1. You run with a kite to catch the air currents which get the kite up in the air. The wind pushing against the kite's surface is what causes it to lift.

2. Observations will vary depending on the difficulties students encountered in building the kite, the weather when they flew it, and the techniques used when launching and flying the kite. Some possibilities include that the length of the bridle affected how easy or difficult it was to launch the kite; that tissue paper kites are fragile and need to be constructed and handled with care; that kites are difficult to fly if the wind is too strong, too light, or if the air is too damp; that launching the kite is more difficult than flying it once altitude is achieved; that the amount of tension kept on the kite string affects how swiftly the kite rises and falls; that the kite can be made to dip by varying this tension. Students may observe that the amount of wind is often different at the surface than it is higher up.

★ ACTIVITY 8

1. Observations will vary depending on the ways that students manipulated the elevators and rudders of the various planes. Look for evidence that the students made adjustments and recorded what happened with each one.

★ ACTIVITY 9

1. The weather is usually fine when the barometer is up. The weather is cloudy or rainy when the barometer is down. When the barometer is in the middle, it usually means the weather is going to change.

2. Tying the balloon to the jar keeps additional air from entering it so that the diaphragm formed from the balloon will move up and down as the pressure changes.

3. Answers will vary depending on weather conditions. If high or low pressure systems move through, readings will vary more than if slow-moving or stationary fronts are present.

4. Air pressure moves the rubber diaphragm, which forces the straw to move up and down.

5. Answers may vary. Scientists generally believe that people are "in a better mood" when barometric pressure is high—possibly because high pressure is associated with fair weather.

★ ACTIVITY 10

1. Answers will vary but will probably be from one-half to three-fourths cup.

2. Answers will vary. Students might note that the peanut butter made using a blender is smoother, while the hand-rolled variety is more like crunchy style peanut butter. Making peanut butter with a blender is easier and faster. Students might observe that almost anything done the old-fashioned way takes longer. Taste will be a matter of personal preference.

3. Adding honey to the peanut butter not only makes it sweeter, but also has a slight emulsifying action. Peanut butter with honey may be less likely to separate.

4. Answers will vary. Commercial peanut butter may be more uniform and sweeter. Students' peanut butter may taste more like fresh peanuts.

5. It made it more popular.

★ ACTIVITY 11

1. Dried food is taken into space because it takes up little room and does not require refrigeration.

2. Answers will vary, but students' results should contain specific examples. Depending on how thinly the foods are sliced, times may vary considerably.

3. Answers will vary, but students will generally find that the "wetter" the food, the longer the drying times. Bananas and apples for example, will dry more quickly than juicier fruits, provided they are thinly sliced.

4. Food plays an important part in the astronauts' morale.

5. Activity reports will vary depending on the foods students chose to dry, the thickness of the slices, the care they took with the process, and the weather. Reports should cover the suggested topics.